Co

MW01534948

Recipe Journal

This Journal belongs to :

_____

Nr	Cocktail Name	Rating
1		☆☆☆☆☆
2		☆☆☆☆☆
3		☆☆☆☆☆
4		☆☆☆☆☆
5		☆☆☆☆☆
6		☆☆☆☆☆
7		☆☆☆☆☆
8		☆☆☆☆☆
9		☆☆☆☆☆
10		☆☆☆☆☆
11		☆☆☆☆☆
12		☆☆☆☆☆
13		☆☆☆☆☆
14		☆☆☆☆☆
15		☆☆☆☆☆
16		☆☆☆☆☆
17		☆☆☆☆☆
18		☆☆☆☆☆
19		☆☆☆☆☆
20		☆☆☆☆☆
21		☆☆☆☆☆
22		☆☆☆☆☆
23		☆☆☆☆☆
24		☆☆☆☆☆
25		☆☆☆☆☆

Nr	Cocktail Name	Rating
26		☆☆☆☆☆
27		☆☆☆☆☆
28		☆☆☆☆☆
29		☆☆☆☆☆
30		☆☆☆☆☆
31		☆☆☆☆☆
32		☆☆☆☆☆
33		☆☆☆☆☆
34		☆☆☆☆☆
35		☆☆☆☆☆
36		☆☆☆☆☆
37		☆☆☆☆☆
38		☆☆☆☆☆
39		☆☆☆☆☆
40		☆☆☆☆☆
41		☆☆☆☆☆
42		☆☆☆☆☆
43		☆☆☆☆☆
44		☆☆☆☆☆
45		☆☆☆☆☆
46		☆☆☆☆☆
47		☆☆☆☆☆
48		☆☆☆☆☆
49		☆☆☆☆☆
50		☆☆☆☆☆

Nr	Cocktail Name	Rating
51		☆☆☆☆☆
52		☆☆☆☆☆
53		☆☆☆☆☆
54		☆☆☆☆☆
55		☆☆☆☆☆
56		☆☆☆☆☆
57		☆☆☆☆☆
58		☆☆☆☆☆
59		☆☆☆☆☆
60		☆☆☆☆☆
61		☆☆☆☆☆
62		☆☆☆☆☆
63		☆☆☆☆☆
64		☆☆☆☆☆
65		☆☆☆☆☆
66		☆☆☆☆☆
67		☆☆☆☆☆
68		☆☆☆☆☆
69		☆☆☆☆☆
70		☆☆☆☆☆
71		☆☆☆☆☆
72		☆☆☆☆☆
73		☆☆☆☆☆
74		☆☆☆☆☆
75		☆☆☆☆☆

Nr	Cocktail Name	Rating
76		☆☆☆☆☆
77		☆☆☆☆☆
78		☆☆☆☆☆
79		☆☆☆☆☆
80		☆☆☆☆☆
81		☆☆☆☆☆
82		☆☆☆☆☆
83		☆☆☆☆☆
84		☆☆☆☆☆
85		☆☆☆☆☆
86		☆☆☆☆☆
87		☆☆☆☆☆
88		☆☆☆☆☆
89		☆☆☆☆☆
90		☆☆☆☆☆
91		☆☆☆☆☆
92		☆☆☆☆☆
93		☆☆☆☆☆
94		☆☆☆☆☆
95		☆☆☆☆☆
96		☆☆☆☆☆
97		☆☆☆☆☆
98		☆☆☆☆☆
99		☆☆☆☆☆
100		☆☆☆☆☆

Date:
_____

Name of the
drink:_____

Difficulty ○ ○ ○ ○ ○

Ingredients:_____
_____
_____
_____
_____
_____

Instructions:_____
_____
_____
_____
_____
_____

Decorations:_____
_____
_____
_____
_____
_____

Rating

☆ ☆ ☆ ☆ ☆

Notes:_____
_____
_____
_____
_____

1

Date:
_____

Name of the
drink:_____

Difficulty ○ ○ ○ ○ ○

Ingredients:_____
_____
_____
_____
_____
_____
_____

Instructions:_____
_____
_____
_____
_____
_____
_____

Decorations:_____
_____
_____
_____
_____
_____
_____

Rating
☆ ☆ ☆ ☆ ☆

Notes:_____
_____
_____
_____
_____

Date:
_____

Name of the
drink:_____

Difficulty ○ ○ ○ ○ ○

Ingredients:_____

_____

_____

_____

_____

_____

_____

Instructions:_____

_____

_____

_____

_____

_____

_____

Decorations:_____

_____

_____

_____

_____

_____

_____

Rating

Notes:_____

_____

_____

_____

_____

_____

Date:
_____

Name of the
drink:_____

Difficulty ○ ○ ○ ○ ○

Ingredients:_____
_____
_____
_____
_____
_____
_____

Instructions:_____
_____
_____
_____
_____
_____
_____

Decorations:_____
_____
_____
_____
_____
_____
_____

Rating

Notes:_____
_____
_____
_____
_____
_____

4

Date:
_____

Name of the
drink:_____
Difficulty   ◯   ◯   ◯   ◯   ◯

Ingredients:_____
_____
_____
_____
_____
_____
_____

Instructions:_____
_____
_____
_____
_____
_____
_____

Decorations:_____
_____
_____
_____
_____
_____
_____

Rating
☆ ☆ ☆ ☆ ☆

Notes:_____
_____
_____
_____
_____
_____

Date: _____

Name of the
drink:_____

Difficulty ○ ○ ○ ○ ○

Ingredients:_____
_____
_____
_____
_____
_____
_____

Instructions:_____
_____
_____
_____
_____
_____
_____

Decorations:_____
_____
_____
_____
_____
_____
_____

Rating
☆ ☆ ☆ ☆ ☆

Notes:_____
_____
_____
_____
_____
_____

Date:
_____

Name of the
drink:_____

Difficulty ○ ○ ○ ○ ○

Ingredients:_____
_____
_____
_____
_____
_____
_____

Instructions:_____
_____
_____
_____
_____
_____

Decorations:_____
_____
_____
_____
_____
_____
_____

Rating
☆ ☆ ☆ ☆ ☆

Notes:_____
_____
_____
_____
_____
_____

7

Date:
_____

Name of the
drink:_____
Difficulty ○ ○ ○ ○ ○

Ingredients:_____
_____
_____
_____
_____
_____
_____

Instructions:_____
_____
_____
_____
_____
_____

Decorations:_____
_____
_____
_____
_____
_____

Rating
☆ ☆ ☆ ☆ ☆

Notes:_____
_____
_____
_____
_____
_____

Date:
_____

Name of the
drink:_____

Difficulty ○ ○ ○ ○ ○

Ingredients:_____
_____
_____
_____
_____
_____
_____

Instructions:_____
_____
_____
_____
_____
_____
_____

Decorations:_____
_____
_____
_____
_____
_____
_____

Rating

Notes:_____
_____
_____
_____
_____
_____

9

Date:
_____

Name of the
drink:_____

Difficulty ○ ○ ○ ○ ○

Ingredients:_____
_____
_____
_____
_____
_____
_____

Instructions:_____
_____
_____
_____
_____
_____

Decorations:_____
_____
_____
_____
_____
_____

Rating
☆ ☆ ☆ ☆ ☆

Notes:_____
_____
_____
_____
_____

10

Date:
_____

Name of the
drink:_____

Difficulty ○ ○ ○ ○ ○

Ingredients:_____
_____
_____
_____
_____
_____
_____

Instructions:_____
_____
_____
_____
_____
_____
_____

Decorations:_____
_____
_____
_____
_____
_____
_____

Rating
☆ ☆ ☆ ☆ ☆

Notes:_____
_____
_____
_____
_____
_____

11

Date:
_____

Name of the
drink:_____

Difficulty ○ ○ ○ ○ ○

Ingredients:_____
_____
_____
_____
_____
_____
_____

Instructions:_____
_____
_____
_____
_____
_____

Decorations:_____
_____
_____
_____
_____
_____

Rating
☆ ☆ ☆ ☆ ☆

Notes:_____
_____
_____
_____
_____

12

Date:
_____

Name of the
drink:_____
Difficulty ○ ○ ○ ○ ○

Ingredients:_____
_____
_____
_____
_____
_____
_____

Instructions:_____
_____
_____
_____
_____
_____
_____

Decorations:_____
_____
_____
_____
_____
_____
_____

Rating
☆ ☆ ☆ ☆ ☆

Notes:_____
_____
_____
_____
_____

13

Date:
_____

Name of the
drink:_____

Difficulty ○ ○ ○ ○ ○

Ingredients:_____
_____
_____
_____
_____
_____
_____

Instructions:_____
_____
_____
_____
_____
_____
_____

Decorations:_____
_____
_____
_____
_____
_____
_____

Rating

☆ ☆ ☆ ☆ ☆

Notes:_____
_____
_____
_____
_____

Date:
_____

Name of the
drink:_____
Difficulty ○ ○ ○ ○ ○

Ingredients:_____
_____
_____
_____
_____
_____
_____

Instructions:_____
_____
_____
_____
_____
_____
_____

Decorations:_____
_____
_____
_____
_____
_____
_____

Rating
☆ ☆ ☆ ☆ ☆

Notes:_____
_____
_____
_____
_____
_____

15

Date:
_____

Name of the
drink:_____
Difficulty ○ ○ ○ ○ ○

Ingredients:_____
_____
_____
_____
_____
_____
_____

Instructions:_____
_____
_____
_____
_____
_____
_____

Decorations:_____
_____
_____
_____
_____
_____
_____

Rating

Notes:_____
_____
_____
_____
_____

Date:
_____

Name of the
drink:_____

Difficulty ○ ○ ○ ○ ○

Ingredients:_____
_____
_____
_____
_____
_____
_____

Instructions:_____
_____
_____
_____
_____
_____
_____

Decorations:_____
_____
_____
_____
_____
_____
_____

Rating
☆ ☆ ☆ ☆ ☆

Notes:_____
_____
_____
_____
_____
_____

17

Date:

_____

Name of the
drink:_____

Difficulty ○ ○ ○ ○ ○

Ingredients:_____

_____

_____

_____

_____

_____

_____

Instructions:_____

_____

_____

_____

_____

_____

Decorations:_____

_____

_____

_____

_____

_____

Rating

☆ ☆ ☆ ☆ ☆

Notes:_____

_____

_____

_____

_____

Date:

_____

Name of the
drink:_____

Difficulty ○ ○ ○ ○ ○

Ingredients:_____

_____

_____

_____

_____

_____

_____

Instructions:_____

_____

_____

_____

_____

_____

_____

Decorations:_____

_____

_____

_____

_____

_____

_____

Rating

☆ ☆ ☆ ☆ ☆

Notes:_____

_____

_____

_____

_____

_____

19

Date:
_____

Name of the
drink:_____

Difficulty ○ ○ ○ ○ ○

Ingredients:_____
_____
_____
_____
_____
_____
_____

Instructions:_____
_____
_____
_____
_____
_____

Decorations:_____
_____
_____
_____
_____
_____

Rating
☆ ☆ ☆ ☆ ☆

Notes:_____
_____
_____
_____
_____
_____

20

Date:
_____

Name of the
drink:_____

Difficulty ○ ○ ○ ○ ○

Ingredients:_____
_____
_____
_____
_____
_____
_____

Instructions:_____
_____
_____
_____
_____
_____
_____

Decorations:_____
_____
_____
_____
_____
_____
_____

Rating

☆ ☆ ☆ ☆ ☆

Notes:_____
_____
_____
_____
_____

Date:
_____

Name of the
drink:_____

Difficulty ○ ○ ○ ○ ○

Ingredients:_____
_____
_____
_____
_____
_____
_____

Instructions:_____
_____
_____
_____
_____
_____
_____

Decorations:_____
_____
_____
_____
_____
_____
_____

Rating

Notes:_____
_____
_____
_____
_____
_____

Date:
_____

Name of the
drink:_____

Difficulty ○ ○ ○ ○ ○

Ingredients:_____
_____
_____
_____
_____
_____
_____

Instructions:_____
_____
_____
_____
_____
_____
_____

Decorations:_____
_____
_____
_____
_____
_____
_____

Rating
☆ ☆ ☆ ☆ ☆

Notes:_____
_____
_____
_____
_____

Date:
_____

Name of the
drink:_____

Difficulty ○ ○ ○ ○ ○

Ingredients:_____
_____
_____
_____
_____
_____
_____

Instructions:_____
_____
_____
_____
_____
_____
_____

Decorations:_____
_____
_____
_____
_____
_____
_____

Rating

Notes:_____
_____
_____
_____
_____
_____

Date:
_____

Name of the
drink:_____
Difficulty ○ ○ ○ ○ ○

Ingredients:_____
_____
_____
_____
_____
_____
_____

Instructions:_____
_____
_____
_____
_____
_____
_____

Decorations:_____
_____
_____
_____
_____
_____
_____

Rating
☆ ☆ ☆ ☆ ☆

Notes:_____
_____
_____
_____
_____

25

Date:
_____

Name of the
drink:_____

Difficulty ○ ○ ○ ○ ○

Ingredients:_____
_____
_____
_____
_____
_____
_____

Instructions:_____
_____
_____
_____
_____
_____

Decorations:_____
_____
_____
_____
_____
_____

Rating
☆ ☆ ☆ ☆ ☆

Notes:_____
_____
_____
_____
_____

26

Date:_____

Name of the
drink:_____
Difficulty ○ ○ ○ ○ ○

Ingredients:_____
_____
_____
_____
_____
_____
_____

Instructions:_____
_____
_____
_____
_____
_____
_____

Decorations:_____
_____
_____
_____
_____
_____
_____

Rating
☆ ☆ ☆ ☆ ☆

Notes:_____
_____
_____
_____
_____

Date:
_____

Name of the
drink:_____

Difficulty ○ ○ ○ ○ ○

Ingredients:_____
_____
_____
_____
_____
_____
_____

Instructions:_____
_____
_____
_____
_____
_____
_____

Decorations:_____
_____
_____
_____
_____
_____
_____

Rating
☆ ☆ ☆ ☆ ☆

Notes:_____
_____
_____
_____
_____
_____

Date:

_____

Name of the
drink:_____

Difficulty ◯ ◯ ◯ ◯ ◯

Ingredients:_____
_____
_____
_____
_____
_____
_____

Instructions:_____
_____
_____
_____
_____
_____
_____

Decorations:_____
_____
_____
_____
_____
_____
_____

Rating
☆ ☆ ☆ ☆ ☆

Notes:_____
_____
_____
_____
_____

Date:
_____

Name of the
drink:_____

Difficulty ○ ○ ○ ○ ○

Ingredients:_____
_____
_____
_____
_____
_____
_____

Instructions:_____
_____
_____
_____
_____
_____
_____

Decorations:_____
_____
_____
_____
_____
_____
_____

Rating
☆ ☆ ☆ ☆ ☆

Notes:_____
_____
_____
_____
_____
_____

30

Date:
_____

Name of the
drink:_____
      Difficulty ○ ○ ○ ○ ○

Ingredients:_____
_____
_____
_____
_____
_____
_____

Instructions:_____
_____
_____
_____
_____
_____
_____

Decorations:_____
_____
_____
_____
_____
_____
_____

Rating
☆ ☆ ☆ ☆ ☆

Notes:_____
_____
_____
_____
_____

Date:
_____

Name of the
drink:_____

Difficulty ◯ ◯ ◯ ◯ ◯

Ingredients:_____
_____
_____
_____
_____
_____
_____

Instructions:_____
_____
_____
_____
_____
_____
_____

Decorations:_____
_____
_____
_____
_____
_____
_____

Rating

Notes:_____
_____
_____
_____
_____
_____

Date:
_____

Name of the
drink:_____

Difficulty ○ ○ ○ ○ ○

Ingredients:_____
_____
_____
_____
_____
_____
_____

Instructions:_____
_____
_____
_____
_____
_____
_____

Decorations:_____
_____
_____
_____
_____
_____
_____

Rating
☆ ☆ ☆ ☆ ☆

Notes:_____
_____
_____
_____
_____
_____

Date:
_____

Name of the
drink:_____

Difficulty ○ ○ ○ ○ ○

Ingredients:_____
_____
_____
_____
_____
_____
_____

Instructions:_____
_____
_____
_____
_____
_____
_____

Decorations:_____
_____
_____
_____
_____
_____
_____

Rating

☆ ☆ ☆ ☆ ☆

Notes:_____
_____
_____
_____
_____
_____

34

Date:
_____

Name of the
drink:_____

Difficulty ◯ ◯ ◯ ◯ ◯

Ingredients:_____
_____
_____
_____
_____
_____
_____

Instructions:_____
_____
_____
_____
_____
_____
_____

Decorations:_____
_____
_____
_____
_____
_____
_____

Rating
☆ ☆ ☆ ☆ ☆

Notes:_____
_____
_____
_____
_____
_____

35

Date:
_____

Name of the
drink:_____

Difficulty ○ ○ ○ ○ ○

Ingredients:_____,_____
_____
_____
_____
_____
_____
_____

Instructions:_____
_____
_____
_____
_____
_____

Decorations:_____
_____
_____
_____
_____
_____

Rating
☆ ☆ ☆ ☆ ☆

Notes:_____
_____
_____
_____
_____

Date:
_____

Name of the
drink:_____

Difficulty ◯ ◯ ◯ ◯ ◯

Ingredients:_____
_____
_____
_____
_____
_____
_____

Instructions:_____
_____
_____
_____
_____
_____
_____

Decorations:_____
_____
_____
_____
_____
_____
_____

Rating

Notes:_____
_____
_____
_____
_____

Date:
_____

Name of the
drink:_____

Difficulty ○ ○ ○ ○ ○

Ingredients:_____

_____

_____

_____

_____

_____

_____

Instructions:_____

_____

_____

_____

_____

_____

_____

Decorations:_____

_____

_____

_____

_____

_____

_____

Rating

Notes:_____

_____

_____

_____

_____

_____

38

Date:
_____

Name of the
drink:_____

Difficulty ◯ ◯ ◯ ◯ ◯

Ingredients:_____
_____
_____
_____
_____
_____
_____

Instructions:_____
_____
_____
_____
_____
_____
_____

Decorations:_____
_____
_____
_____
_____
_____
_____

Rating

Notes:_____
_____
_____
_____
_____
_____

39

Date:

_____

Name of the
drink:_____

Difficulty ○ ○ ○ ○ ○

Ingredients:_____

_____

_____

_____

_____

_____

_____

Instructions:_____

_____

_____

_____

_____

_____

_____

Decorations:_____

_____

_____

_____

_____

_____

_____

Rating

Notes:_____

_____

_____

_____

_____

_____

Date:
_____

Name of the
drink:_____

Difficulty ○ ○ ○ ○ ○

Ingredients:_____
_____
_____
_____
_____
_____
_____

Instructions:_____
_____
_____
_____
_____
_____
_____

Decorations:_____
_____
_____
_____
_____
_____
_____

Rating
☆ ☆ ☆ ☆ ☆

Notes:_____
_____
_____
_____
_____
_____

Date:_____

Name of the
drink:_____

Difficulty ○ ○ ○ ○ ○

Ingredients:_____
_____
_____
_____
_____
_____
_____

Instructions:_____
_____
_____
_____
_____
_____

Decorations:_____
_____
_____
_____
_____
_____

Rating

☆ ☆ ☆ ☆ ☆

Notes:_____
_____
_____
_____
_____

42

Date:
_____

Name of the
drink:_____
          Difficulty ○ ○ ○ ○ ○

Ingredients:_____
_____
_____
_____
_____
_____
_____

Instructions:_____
_____
_____
_____
_____
_____
_____

Decorations:_____
_____
_____
_____
_____
_____
_____   Rating
              ☆ ☆ ☆ ☆ ☆

Notes:_____
_____
_____
_____
_____
_____

43

Date:

_____

Name of the
drink:_____

Difficulty ○ ○ ○ ○ ○

Ingredients:_____

_____

_____

_____

_____

_____

_____

Instructions:_____

_____

_____

_____

_____

_____

Decorations:_____

_____

_____

_____

_____

_____

Rating

☆ ☆ ☆ ☆ ☆

Notes:_____

_____

_____

_____

_____

44

Date:
_____

Name of the
drink:_____

Difficulty ○ ○ ○ ○ ○

Ingredients:_____

_____

_____

_____

_____

_____

_____

Instructions:_____

_____

_____

_____

_____

_____

Decorations:_____

_____

_____

_____

_____

_____   Rating

☆ ☆ ☆ ☆ ☆

Notes:_____

_____

_____

_____

_____

_____

45

Date:
_____

Name of the
drink:_____

Difficulty ○ ○ ○ ○ ○

Ingredients:_____
_____
_____
_____
_____
_____
_____

Instructions:_____
_____
_____
_____
_____
_____
_____

Decorations:_____
_____
_____
_____
_____
_____
_____

Rating

Notes:_____
_____
_____
_____
_____

Date:
_____

Name of the
drink:_____

Difficulty ◯ ◯ ◯ ◯ ◯

Ingredients:_____
_____
_____
_____
_____
_____
_____

Instructions:_____
_____
_____
_____
_____
_____
_____

Decorations:_____
_____
_____
_____
_____
_____
_____

Rating

☆ ☆ ☆ ☆ ☆

Notes:_____
_____
_____
_____
_____

Date:
_____

Name of the
drink:_____

Difficulty ○ ○ ○ ○ ○

Ingredients:_____

_____

_____

_____

_____

_____

_____

Instructions:__________

_____

_____

_____

_____

_____

Decorations:_____

_____

_____

_____

_____

_____

Rating

☆ ☆ ☆ ☆ ☆

Notes:_____

_____

_____

_____

_____

Date:_____

Name of the
drink:_____

Difficulty ○ ○ ○ ○ ○

Ingredients:_____
_____
_____
_____
_____
_____

Instructions:_____
_____
_____
_____
_____
_____

Decorations:_____
_____
_____
_____
_____
_____

Rating

Notes:_____
_____
_____
_____
_____
_____

Date:

Name of the
drink:

Difficulty ○ ○ ○ ○ ○

Ingredients:

Instructions:

Decorations:

Rating
☆ ☆ ☆ ☆ ☆

Notes:

50

Date:
_____

Name of the
drink:_____

Difficulty ○ ○ ○ ○ ○

Ingredients:_____

_____
_____
_____
_____
_____
_____

Instructions:_____

_____
_____
_____
_____
_____
_____

Decorations:_____

_____
_____
_____
_____
_____
_____

Rating
☆ ☆ ☆ ☆ ☆

Notes:_____

_____
_____
_____
_____
_____

Date:

Name of the
drink:

Difficulty ○ ○ ○ ○ ○

Ingredients:

Instructions:

Decorations:

Rating

Notes:

52

Date:

_____

Name of the
drink:_____

Difficulty ○ ○ ○ ○ ○

Ingredients:_____
_____
_____
_____
_____
_____
_____

Instructions:_____
_____
_____
_____
_____
_____
_____

Decorations:_____
_____
_____
_____
_____
_____
_____

Rating
☆ ☆ ☆ ☆ ☆

Notes:_____
_____
_____
_____
_____

53

Date:
_____

Name of the
drink:_____

Difficulty ○ ○ ○ ○ ○

Ingredients:_____
_____
_____
_____
_____
_____
_____

Instructions:_____
_____
_____
_____
_____
_____
_____

Decorations:_____
_____
_____
_____
_____
_____
_____

Rating
☆ ☆ ☆ ☆ ☆

Notes:_____
_____
_____
_____
_____
_____

54

Date:_____

Name of the
drink:_____

Difficulty ○ ○ ○ ○ ○

Ingredients:_____
_____
_____
_____
_____
_____
_____

Instructions:_____
_____
_____
_____
_____
_____
_____

Decorations:_____
_____
_____
_____
_____
_____
_____

Rating

Notes:_____
_____
_____
_____
_____
_____

Date:
_____

Name of the
drink:_____

Difficulty ○ ○ ○ ○ ○

Ingredients:_____
_____
_____
_____
_____
_____
_____
Instructions:_____
_____
_____
_____
_____
_____
_____
Decorations:_____
_____
_____
_____
_____
_____
_____

Rating

Notes:_____
_____
_____
_____
_____
_____

Date:
_____

Name of the
drink:_____

Difficulty ○ ○ ○ ○ ○

Ingredients:_____
_____
_____
_____
_____
_____
_____

Instructions:_____
_____
_____
_____
_____
_____
_____

Decorations:_____
_____
_____
_____
_____
_____
_____

Rating
☆ ☆ ☆ ☆ ☆

Notes:_____
_____
_____
_____
_____

Date:
_____

Name of the
drink:_____

Difficulty ○ ○ ○ ○ ○

Ingredients:_____
_____
_____
_____
_____
_____
_____

Instructions:_____
_____
_____
_____
_____
_____
_____

Decorations:_____
_____
_____
_____
_____
_____
_____

Rating

Notes:_____
_____
_____
_____
_____

58

Date:
_____

Name of the
drink:_____

Difficulty ○ ○ ○ ○ ○

Ingredients:_____
_____
_____
_____
_____
_____
_____

Instructions:_____
_____
_____
_____
_____
_____
_____

Decorations:_____
_____
_____
_____
_____
_____
_____

Rating
☆ ☆ ☆ ☆ ☆

Notes:_____
_____
_____
_____
_____

59

Date:
_____

Name of the
drink:_____
Difficulty ○ ○ ○ ○ ○

Ingredients:_____
_____
_____
_____
_____
_____
_____

Instructions:_____
_____
_____
_____
_____
_____
_____

Decorations:_____
_____
_____
_____
_____
_____
_____

Rating
☆ ☆ ☆ ☆ ☆

Notes:_____
_____
_____
_____
_____
_____

60

Date:
_____

Name of the
drink:_____

Difficulty ○ ○ ○ ○ ○

Ingredients:_____
_____
_____
_____
_____
_____
_____

Instructions:_____
_____
_____
_____
_____
_____
_____

Decorations:_____
_____
_____
_____
_____
_____
_____

Rating

Notes:_____
_____
_____
_____
_____
_____

Date:
_____

Name of the
drink:_____

Difficulty   ◯   ◯   ◯   ◯   ◯

Ingredients:_____
_____
_____
_____
_____
_____
_____

Instructions:_____
_____
_____
_____
_____
_____

Decorations:_____
_____
_____
_____
_____
_____

Rating
☆   ☆   ☆   ☆   ☆

Notes:_____
_____
_____
_____
_____

62

Date:
_____

Name of the
drink:_____

Difficulty ○ ○ ○ ○ ○

Ingredients:_____
_____
_____
_____
_____
_____
_____

Instructions:_____
_____
_____
_____
_____
_____
_____

Decorations:_____
_____
_____
_____
_____
_____
_____

Rating

Notes:_____
_____
_____
_____
_____

63

Date:
_____

Name of the
drink:_____

Difficulty ○ ○ ○ ○ ○

Ingredients:_____

_____

_____

_____

_____

_____

_____

Instructions:_____

_____

_____

_____

_____

_____

_____

Decorations:_____

_____

_____

_____

_____

_____

_____

Rating

Notes:_____

_____

_____

_____

_____

_____

64

Date:
_____

Name of the
drink:_____

Difficulty ◯ ◯ ◯ ◯ ◯

Ingredients:_____
_____
_____
_____
_____
_____
_____

Instructions:_____
_____
_____
_____
_____
_____
_____

Decorations:_____
_____
_____
_____
_____
_____
_____

Rating

Notes:_____
_____
_____
_____
_____
_____

65

Date:
_____

Name of the
drink:_____

Difficulty ○ ○ ○ ○ ○

Ingredients:_____
_____
_____
_____
_____
_____
_____

Instructions:_____
_____
_____
_____
_____
_____
_____

Decorations:_____
_____
_____
_____
_____
_____
_____

Rating
☆ ☆ ☆ ☆ ☆

Notes:_____
_____
_____
_____
_____
_____

66

Date:
_____

Name of the
drink:_____

Difficulty ○ ○ ○ ○ ○

Ingredients:_____
_____
_____
_____
_____
_____
_____

Instructions:_____
_____
_____
_____
_____
_____
_____

Decorations:_____
_____
_____
_____
_____
_____
_____

Rating
☆ ☆ ☆ ☆ ☆

Notes:_____
_____
_____
_____
_____

67

Date:
_____

Name of the
drink:_____

Difficulty ○ ○ ○ ○ ○

Ingredients:_____
_____
_____
_____
_____
_____
_____

Instructions:_____
_____
_____
_____
_____
_____

Decorations:_____
_____
_____
_____
_____
_____

Rating
☆ ☆ ☆ ☆ ☆

Notes:_____
_____
_____
_____
_____

68

Date:
_____

Name of the
drink:_____

Difficulty ○ ○ ○ ○ ○

Ingredients:_____
_____
_____
_____
_____
_____
_____

Instructions:_____
_____
_____
_____
_____
_____
_____

Decorations:_____
_____
_____
_____
_____
_____
_____

Rating
☆ ☆ ☆ ☆ ☆

Notes:_____
_____
_____
_____
_____
_____

69

Date:

_____

Name of the
drink:_____

Difficulty ○ ○ ○ ○ ○

Ingredients:_____
_____
_____
_____
_____
_____
_____

Instructions:_____
_____
_____
_____
_____
_____

Decorations:_____
_____
_____
_____
_____
_____

Rating

☆ ☆ ☆ ☆ ☆

Notes:_____
_____
_____
_____
_____

70

Date:
_____

Name of the
drink:_____

Difficulty ○ ○ ○ ○ ○

Ingredients:_____
_____
_____
_____
_____
_____
_____

Instructions:_____
_____
_____
_____
_____
_____
_____

Decorations:_____
_____
_____
_____
_____
_____
_____

Rating

Notes:_____
_____
_____
_____
_____
_____

Date:

_____

Name of the
drink:_____

Difficulty ○ ○ ○ ○ ○

Ingredients:_____
_____
_____
_____
_____
_____
_____

Instructions:_____
_____
_____
_____
_____
_____

Decorations:_____
_____
_____
_____
_____
_____

Rating

☆ ☆ ☆ ☆ ☆

Notes:_____
_____
_____
_____
_____
_____

72

Date:
_____

Name of the
drink:_____

Difficulty ○ ○ ○ ○ ○

Ingredients:_____
_____
_____
_____
_____
_____
_____

Instructions:_____
_____
_____
_____
_____
_____
_____

Decorations:_____
_____
_____
_____
_____
_____
_____

Rating
☆ ☆ ☆ ☆ ☆

Notes:_____
_____
_____
_____
_____

73

Date:
_____

Name of the
drink:_____

Difficulty ○ ○ ○ ○ ○

Ingredients:_____

_____

_____

_____

_____

_____

_____

Instructions:_____

_____

_____

_____

_____

_____

Decorations:_____

_____

_____

_____

_____

_____

Rating

☆ ☆ ☆ ☆ ☆

Notes:_____

_____

_____

_____

_____

_____

74

Date:
_____

Name of the
drink:_____

Difficulty ○ ○ ○ ○ ○

Ingredients:_____
_____
_____
_____
_____
_____
_____

Instructions:_____
_____
_____
_____
_____
_____
_____

Decorations:_____
_____
_____
_____
_____
_____
_____

Rating
☆ ☆ ☆ ☆ ☆

Notes:_____
_____
_____
_____
_____

75

Date:
_____

Name of the
drink:_____

Difficulty ○ ○ ○ ○ ○

Ingredients:_____
_____
_____
_____
_____
_____
_____

Instructions:_____
_____
_____
_____
_____
_____
_____

Decorations:_____
_____
_____
_____
_____
_____
_____

Rating
☆ ☆ ☆ ☆ ☆

Notes:_____
_____
_____
_____
_____
_____

76

Date:
_____

Name of the
drink:_____

Difficulty ○ ○ ○ ○ ○

Ingredients:_____
_____
_____
_____
_____
_____
_____

Instructions:_____
_____
_____
_____
_____
_____
_____

Decorations:_____
_____
_____
_____
_____
_____
_____

Rating
☆ ☆ ☆ ☆ ☆

Notes:_____
_____
_____
_____
_____
_____

77

Date:_____

Name of the
drink:_____

Difficulty ○ ○ ○ ○ ○

Ingredients:_____
_____
_____
_____
_____
_____
_____

Instructions:_____
_____
_____
_____
_____
_____
_____

Decorations:_____
_____
_____
_____
_____
_____
_____

Rating
☆ ☆ ☆ ☆ ☆

Notes:_____
_____
_____
_____
_____
_____

78

Date:_____

Name of the
drink:_____

Difficulty ○ ○ ○ ○ ○

Ingredients:_____
_____
_____
_____
_____
_____
_____

Instructions:_____
_____
_____
_____
_____
_____
_____

Decorations:_____
_____
_____
_____
_____
_____

Rating

Notes:_____
_____
_____
_____
_____

Date:
_____

Name of the
drink:_____

Difficulty ○ ○ ○ ○ ○

Ingredients:_____
_____
_____
_____
_____
_____
_____

Instructions:_____
_____
_____
_____
_____
_____

Decorations:_____
_____
_____
_____
_____
_____

Rating

Notes:_____
_____
_____
_____
_____

80

Date:
_____

Name of the
drink:_____

Difficulty ○ ○ ○ ○ ○

Ingredients:_____
_____
_____
_____
_____
_____
_____

Instructions:_____
_____
_____
_____
_____
_____
_____

Decorations:_____
_____
_____
_____
_____
_____
_____

Rating
☆ ☆ ☆ ☆ ☆

Notes:_____
_____
_____
_____
_____
_____

Date:
_____

Name of the
drink:_____

Difficulty ○ ○ ○ ○ ○

Ingredients:_____
_____
_____
_____
_____
_____
_____

Instructions:_____
_____
_____
_____
_____
_____

Decorations:_____
_____
_____
_____
_____
_____
_____

Rating
☆ ☆ ☆ ☆ ☆

Notes:_____
_____
_____
_____
_____
_____

82

Date:
_____

Name of the
drink:_____

Difficulty ○ ○ ○ ○ ○

Ingredients:_____
_____
_____
_____
_____
_____
_____

Instructions:_____
_____
_____
_____
_____
_____
_____

Decorations:_____
_____
_____
_____
_____
_____
_____

Rating
☆ ☆ ☆ ☆ ☆

Notes:_____
_____
_____
_____
_____

83

Date:
_____

Name of the
drink:_____

Difficulty ○ ○ ○ ○ ○

Ingredients:_____
_____
_____
_____
_____
_____
_____

Instructions:_____
_____
_____
_____
_____
_____
_____

Decorations:_____
_____
_____
_____
_____
_____
_____

Rating
☆ ☆ ☆ ☆ ☆

Notes:_____
_____
_____
_____
_____

Date:_____

Name of the
drink:_____

Difficulty ○ ○ ○ ○ ○

Ingredients:_____
_____
_____
_____
_____
_____
_____

Instructions:_____
_____
_____
_____
_____
_____
_____

Decorations:_____
_____
_____
_____
_____
_____
_____

Rating
☆ ☆ ☆ ☆ ☆

Notes:_____
_____
_____
_____
_____
_____

Date:
_____

Name of the
drink:_____

Difficulty ○ ○ ○ ○ ○

Ingredients:_____
_____
_____
_____
_____
_____
_____
Instructions:_____
_____
_____
_____
_____
_____
Decorations:_____
_____
_____
_____
_____
_____
Rating

Notes:_____
_____
_____
_____
_____

Date:
_____

Name of the
drink:_____

Difficulty ○ ○ ○ ○ ○

Ingredients:_____
_____
_____
_____
_____
_____
_____

Instructions:_____
_____
_____
_____
_____
_____
_____

Decorations:_____
_____
_____
_____
_____
_____
_____

Rating

☆ ☆ ☆ ☆ ☆

Notes:_____
_____
_____
_____
_____
_____

Date:

_____

Name of the
drink:_____

Difficulty ○ ○ ○ ○ ○

Ingredients:_____

_____

_____

_____

_____

_____

_____

Instructions:_____

_____

_____

_____

_____

_____

_____

Decorations:_____

_____

_____

_____

_____

_____

_____

Rating

☆ ☆ ☆ ☆ ☆

Notes:_____

_____

_____

_____

_____

_____

88

Date:
_____

Name of the
drink:_____

Difficulty ○ ○ ○ ○ ○

Ingredients:_____
_____
_____
_____
_____
_____
_____

Instructions:_____
_____
_____
_____
_____
_____
_____

Decorations:_____
_____
_____
_____
_____
_____
_____

Rating

Notes:_____
_____
_____
_____
_____
_____

Date:
_____

Name of the
drink:_____

Difficulty ○ ○ ○ ○ ○

Ingredients:_____
_____
_____
_____
_____
_____
_____

Instructions:_____
_____
_____
_____
_____
_____
_____

Decorations:_____
_____
_____
_____
_____
_____
_____

Rating

Notes:_____
_____
_____
_____
_____
_____

Date:
_____

Name of the
drink:_____

Difficulty ○ ○ ○ ○ ○

Ingredients:_____

_____

_____

_____

_____

_____

_____

Instructions:_____

_____

_____

_____

_____

_____

_____

Decorations:_____

_____

_____

_____

_____

_____

_____

Rating

Notes:_____

_____

_____

_____

_____

_____

Date:
_____

Name of the
drink:_____

Difficulty ⚪ ⚪ ⚪ ⚪ ⚪

Ingredients:_____
_____
_____
_____
_____
_____
_____

Instructions:_____
_____
_____
_____
_____
_____
_____

Decorations:_____
_____
_____
_____
_____
_____
_____

Rating
☆ ☆ ☆ ☆ ☆

Notes:_____
_____
_____
_____
_____

Date:
_____

Name of the
drink:_____

Difficulty ◯ ◯ ◯ ◯ ◯

Ingredients:_____
_____
_____
_____
_____
_____
_____

Instructions:_____
_____
_____
_____
_____
_____
_____

Decorations:_____
_____
_____
_____
_____
_____
_____

Rating

☆ ☆ ☆ ☆ ☆

Notes:_____
_____
_____
_____
_____

Date:
_____

Name of the
drink:_____

Difficulty ◯ ◯ ◯ ◯ ◯

Ingredients:_____
_____
_____
_____
_____
_____
_____

Instructions:_____
_____
_____
_____
_____
_____

Decorations:_____
_____
_____
_____
_____
_____

Rating
☆ ☆ ☆ ☆ ☆

Notes:_____
_____
_____
_____
_____
_____

94

Date:
_____

Name of the
drink:_____

Difficulty ○ ○ ○ ○ ○

Ingredients:_____
_____
_____
_____
_____
_____
_____

Instructions:_____
_____
_____
_____
_____
_____
_____

Decorations:_____
_____
_____
_____
_____
_____
_____

Rating

Notes:_____
_____
_____
_____
_____
_____

Date:
_____

Name of the
drink:_____

Difficulty ○ ○ ○ ○ ○

Ingredients:_____
_____
_____
_____
_____
_____
_____

Instructions:_____
_____
_____
_____
_____
_____
_____

Decorations:_____
_____
_____
_____
_____
_____
_____

Rating
☆ ☆ ☆ ☆ ☆

Notes:_____
_____
_____
_____
_____

Date:
_____

Name of the
drink:_____

Difficulty ○ ○ ○ ○ ○

Ingredients:_____
_____
_____
_____
_____
_____
_____

Instructions:_____
_____
_____
_____
_____
_____
_____

Decorations:_____
_____
_____
_____
_____
_____
_____

Rating

Notes:_____
_____
_____
_____
_____
_____

Date:
_____

Name of the
drink:_____
Difficulty ○ ○ ○ ○ ○

Ingredients:_____
_____
_____
_____
_____
_____
_____

Instructions:_____
_____
_____
_____
_____
_____
_____

Decorations:_____
_____
_____
_____
_____
_____
_____

Rating
☆ ☆ ☆ ☆ ☆

Notes:_____
_____
_____
_____
_____

Date:
_____

Name of the
drink:_____
Difficulty ○ ○ ○ ○ ○

Ingredients:_____
_____
_____
_____
_____
_____
_____

Instructions:_____
_____
_____
_____
_____
_____
_____

Decorations:_____
_____
_____
_____
_____
_____
_____

Rating
☆ ☆ ☆ ☆ ☆

Notes:_____
_____
_____
_____
_____
_____

Date:
_____

Name of the
drink:_____

Difficulty ○ ○ ○ ○ ○

Ingredients:_____

_____

_____

_____

_____

_____

_____

Instructions:_____

_____

_____

_____

_____

_____

_____

Decorations:_____

_____

_____

_____

_____

_____

_____

Rating

☆ ☆ ☆ ☆ ☆

Notes:_____

_____

_____

_____

_____

100

CPSIA information can be obtained
at www.ICGtesting.com
Printed in the USA
LVHW051115120221
679116LV00005B/1122

9 781716 123245